OUR
GRE★T
STATES

WHAT'S GREAT ABOUT
KANSAS?

✳ Darice Bailer

LERNER PUBLICATIONS ✳ MINNEAPOLIS

CONTENTS

KANSAS WELCOMES YOU! ✳ 4

Content Consultant: Jay Price, PhD, Professor
of History, Wichita State University

Lerner Publications Company
A division of Lerner Publishing Group, Inc.
241 First Avenue North
Minneapolis, MN 55401 USA

For reading levels and more information, look
up this title at www.lernerbooks.com.

Main body text set in ITC Franklin Gothic Std
Book Condensed 12/15.
Typeface provided by Adobe Systems.

Cataloging-in-Publication Data for *What's
Great about Kansas* is on file at the Library of
Congress.

ISBN: 978-1-4677-3884-2 (lib.)
ISBN: 978-1-4677-8499-3 (pbk.)
ISBN: 978-1-4677-8500-6 (EB pdf)

Manufactured in the United States of America
1 – PC – 7/15/15

KANSAS COSMOSPHERE AND SPACE CENTER ✳ 6

T-BONES BASEBALL ✳ 8

DEANNA ROSE CHILDREN'S FARMSTEAD ✳ 10

GAGE PARK ✳ 12

COMBAT AIR MUSEUM ✳ 14

KANSAS STATE FAIR ✴ 16

T-REX CAFE ✴ 18

STRATACA ✴ 20

WITNESS THE PAST IN WICHITA ✴ 22

STERNBERG MUSEUM ✴ 24

KANSAS BY MAP ✴ 26
KANSAS FACTS ✴ 28
GLOSSARY ✴ 30
FURTHER INFORMATION ✴ 31
INDEX ✴ 32

KANSAS Welcomes You!

Head to Kansas, in the center of the country. Explore real spaceships at the Kansas Cosmosphere and Space Center. Watch baby chicks peck out of their eggs at the state fair. Ride in a horse-drawn wagon in an old frontier town. See cowboys pretend to fight in the dusty street. Walk under the wings of fighter planes. You can even sit at the controls! What other adventures await you? Read on to find out!

Explore Kansas's golden fields and all the places in between! Just turn the page to find out about the **SUNFLOWER STATE.** >

COLORADO

NEBRASKA

Missouri River

SMOKY HILLS

P L A I N S

▲ Mount Sunflower
(4,039 feet/
1,231 m)

N

G R E A T

Manhattan

Shawnee

Kansas City

Topeka

Lenexa

Salina

Kansas River

Lawrence

Overland Park

Olathe

MISSOURI

Little Arkansas River

Arkansas River

Hutchinson

FLINT HILLS

Miles
0   20   40   60
0   40   80
Kilometers

Wichita

OKLAHOMA

KANSAS COSMOSPHERE
AND SPACE CENTER

> Want to see a real moon rock? Visit the Kansas Cosmosphere and Space Center in Hutchinson. American astronauts brought the rock back from their first trip to the moon. Walk through the Mollett Early Space Flight Gallery. Learn more about the history of space travel. Did you know that the United States sent chimpanzees into space? What scientists learned from those trips helped make space travel safer for humans. Check out the real spacecraft that astronauts used for their takeoffs and landings. You can see actual space suits that astronauts wore.

The planetarium and IMAX theater are must-sees. Take a tour of the stars. Watch new movies and cool documentaries on the giant screen! Finish your visit at the rocket show. It's set in a lab from the 1930s. You'll see reenactments of early rocket experiments. Every show ends with a bang!

The Mercury-Redstone rocket on display at the Kansas Cosmosphere and Space Center was used in the Mercury space program.

Take a seat in the Falcon III simulator to feel what it's like to launch and land a space shuttle.

T-BONES BASEBALL

> Would you like to run around the bases at a real ballpark? Take yourself out to the ball game! The Kansas City T-Bones are a minor-league baseball team. The T-Bones home stadium is in CommunityAmerica Park. The playing season usually runs from May through August. After Saturday games, you can enjoy fireworks at the stadium. On Sundays, the team invites kids onto the field. You can run around the bases and touch home plate!
> Bring your mitt to the stadium too. You might catch a foul ball! Don't forget an autograph book. Some of the players will be there to sign.

Bring your mitt and try to catch a foul ball!

WHERE KANSAS GOT ITS NAME

The name Kansas comes from the Kansa American Indians, who lived in what became the state of Kansas. When white settlers came to the area, the Kansa people had to move to government-designated American Indian territory in present-day Oklahoma. In 2014, approximately two thousand people with Kansa ancestors lived in the United States.

DEANNA ROSE

CHILDREN'S FARMSTEAD

The Deanna Rose Children's Farmstead hosts an annual race called the Farmstead Stampede.

> The entrance to the Deanna Rose Children's Farmstead in Overland Park looks like a red barn. The farmstead is just like a farm from the late 1800s! A rooster crows hello. Visit the schoolhouse. It is full of wooden desks. Try to answer the question of the day on the board! How does this school compare to yours?

The metal tractor seats at the farmstead's Cinemoo Theater are a good spot for a rest. Sit down for a movie. Learn how settlers traveled west. After the movie, you can buy a baby bottle filled with milk. Feed the little goats outside. Or toss crumbs to the ducks paddling in the pond! Ponies wait for riders like you. Horses pull passengers on hayrides.

TRAVELING WEST

In the 1800s, many settlers from the eastern United States traveled west. They were looking for a better place to live. Some stopped in Kansas. They were attracted by railroads and cheap land for farming. Sometimes they traveled on horseback or in covered wagons. They also traveled in large groups. The settlers often rode at least 10 miles (16 km) each day. Many slept under the stars.

FARMSTEAD

GAGE PARK

> Head for Gage Park in Topeka, the capital of Kansas. Buy a train ticket at the old red train depot. Take a ride around the park. A mini diesel train blows its whistle. It clacks along the track. Hold your breath through the tunnel! After getting off the train, take a different kind of ride! Spin around on the park's carousel. Pick your favorite hand-carved animal.

The Topeka Zoo is also in the park. See a tiger cub wake up from its nap. Don't miss giraffe feeding time! You can feed lettuce to one of the brown-speckled giraffes. Did you know that a giraffe's tongue is 18 to 22 inches (46 to 56 centimeters) long? Watch its tongue curl and scoop up your food!

See animals up close at the zoo in Gage Park.

The miniature locomotive pulls guests around Gage Park.

COMBAT AIR MUSEUM

> At the Combat Air Museum in Topeka, fighter jets are close enough to touch! The museum has two airplane hangars. They are crowded with real warplanes and helicopters. Look for a ramp into an old US Navy helicopter. The helicopter flew soldiers in wartime. Sit down and buckle up in one of the dark-green seats. Imagine you are on your way to battle. Do you feel ready? Sit in the cockpit of a real fighter jet. Can you figure out the controls?

Pilot oxygen masks and soldier uniforms are on display. Salute any soldiers you see outside. The museum is on an air force base. You might see a flight training drill!

AMELIA EARHART

Amelia Earhart grew up in Kansas. In 1932, she became the first female pilot to fly alone across the Atlantic Ocean. Five years later, she tried to become the first woman to fly around the world. But she and her plane disappeared. Her fate remains a mystery.

Get behind the controls of a fighter jet at the Combat Air Museum.

KANSAS STATE FAIR

> Do you like amusement park rides or animals? Then don't miss the Kansas State Fair in Hutchinson! The fair runs for ten days each September. This fair is huge. But a train or tractor-pulled trolley can take you around the grounds. Newborn lambs or calves take their first steps at the Birthing Center. The fair also has a model of a life-size cow. Try to milk it!

Animals are everywhere at the fair! Pigs race for an Oreo cookie. Donkeys and camels wait to be fed at the petting zoo. Climb a tower and fly across a lake on a zip line. Artists are on hand to paint your face. By now, you must be hungry! Try a chocolate-coated banana. Or grab a corn dog.

Rides like these swings are colorful and fun.

MILK PRODUCTION

It takes about two days for milk to make its way from a cow to the grocery shelf. Cows can produce 8 gallons (30 liters) of milk a day! There are more than 120,000 cows in Kansas. The cows live on approximately three hundred farms around the state.

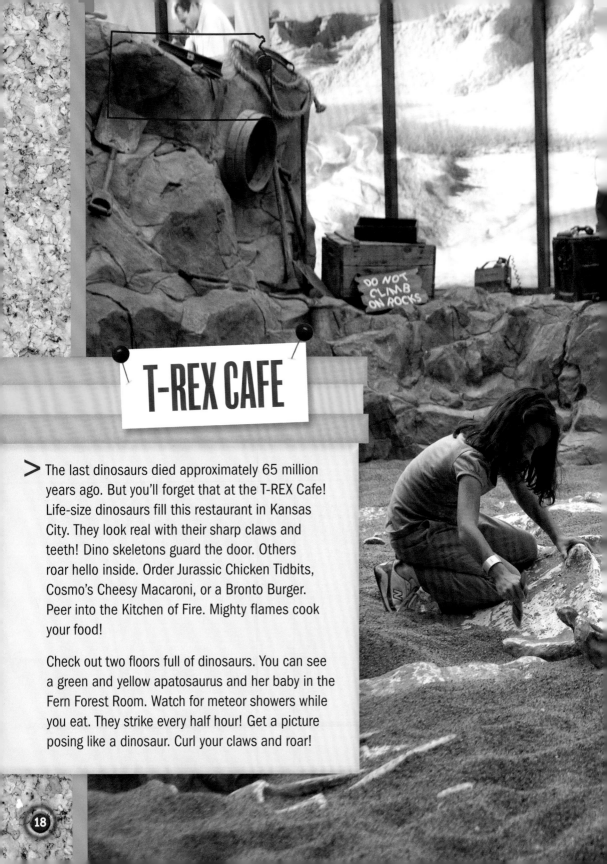

T-REX CAFE

> The last dinosaurs died approximately 65 million years ago. But you'll forget that at the T-REX Cafe! Life-size dinosaurs fill this restaurant in Kansas City. They look real with their sharp claws and teeth! Dino skeletons guard the door. Others roar hello inside. Order Jurassic Chicken Tidbits, Cosmo's Cheesy Macaroni, or a Bronto Burger. Peer into the Kitchen of Fire. Mighty flames cook your food!

Check out two floors full of dinosaurs. You can see a green and yellow apatosaurus and her baby in the Fern Forest Room. Watch for meteor showers while you eat. They strike every half hour! Get a picture posing like a dinosaur. Curl your claws and roar!

DO NOT CLIMB ON ROCKS

Even the entrance of T-REX Cafe displays dinosaur skeletons!

You'll have dinos for dinner companions at the T-REX Cafe!

19

STRATACA

> Have you ever wanted to go deep into the earth? Snap on a hard hat and you can! Go on a tour of Strataca, the Kansas Underground Salt Museum in Hutchinson. The museum is in an old salt mine. Grab a seat on the Salt Mine Express. It's a fifteen-minute train ride through part of the mine. Look for old candy wrappers and magazines. They were left by miners back in the 1940s and the 1950s. There's also a thirty-minute tram ride called the Dark Ride. Travel through a tunnel in total darkness. The walls and the ceiling around you are made of salt!

Check out Harry's Habitat. Harry is a bacterium. It is more than 250 million years old. This bacterium is the oldest living creature on Earth! Look for Harry under a microscope in a crystal of salt. Before you leave, collect a souvenir from the museum. You can take home a rock of salt!

Souvenirs at the underground gift shop include real salt crystals!

WITNESS THE PAST IN WICHITA

Catch a ride in the back of a real horse-drawn wagon.

> American Indians were the first settlers in Kansas and on the Great Plains. At the Mid-America All-Indian Center in Wichita, you can crawl inside a children's tepee. It is a tentlike American Indian dwelling. Listen to a powwow drum. The drum beats out the rhythm to a dance.

Follow a path along the river. It leads to the nearby Old Cowtown Museum. Here you can see what it was like to be a white settler 160 years ago. Pick up one of the pioneer toys outside. You may find a pair of walking sticks. Or roll an old wooden hoop in the dusty street. Ride a horse-drawn wagon past the old shops. Try a bottle of sarsaparilla in the saloon. It tastes like root beer and cream soda. Then grab a seat on the saloon's porch. Don't miss the pretend gunfights in the street!

KEEPER OF THE PLAINS

Look for a tall steel sculpture near the Mid-America All-Indian Center. It's called the Keeper of the Plains. An American Indian artist named Francis "Blackbear" Bosin created the statue. It represents an American Indian chief. The chief stands on a stone base where the Big and Little Arkansas Rivers meet. The Wichita American Indian tribe once built grass houses and tepees here. The city is named after these Great Plains American Indians.

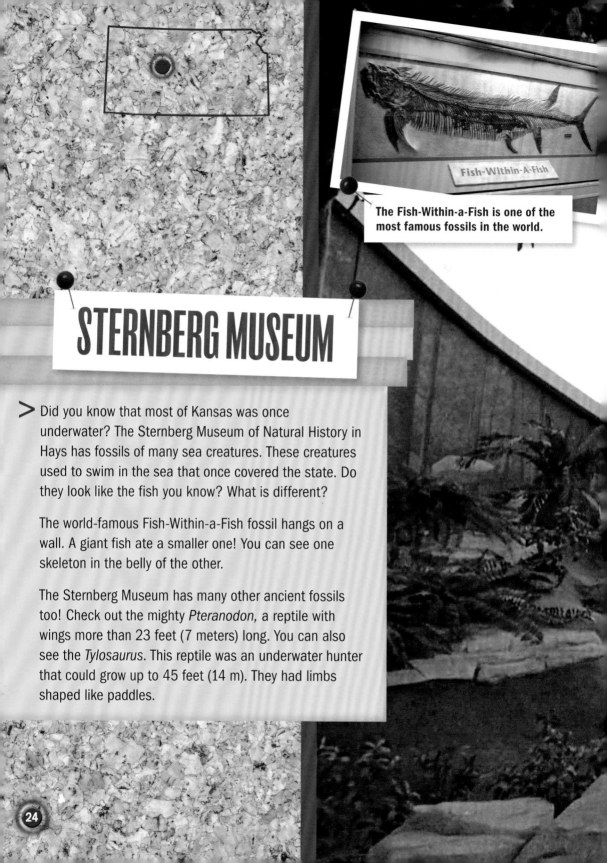

Fish-Within-A-Fish

The Fish-Within-a-Fish is one of the most famous fossils in the world.

STERNBERG MUSEUM

> Did you know that most of Kansas was once underwater? The Sternberg Museum of Natural History in Hays has fossils of many sea creatures. These creatures used to swim in the sea that once covered the state. Do they look like the fish you know? What is different?

The world-famous Fish-Within-a-Fish fossil hangs on a wall. A giant fish ate a smaller one! You can see one skeleton in the belly of the other.

The Sternberg Museum has many other ancient fossils too! Check out the mighty *Pteranodon,* a reptile with wings more than 23 feet (7 meters) long. You can also see the *Tylosaurus.* This reptile was an underwater hunter that could grow up to 45 feet (14 m). They had limbs shaped like paddles.

This fish used to swim over Kansas in an ocean!

YOUR TOP TEN!

You just read about ten great things to see and do in Kansas. If you were planning a trip to Kansas, what would be on your top ten list? What kinds of animals or sights would you like to see? What Kansas activities sound most exciting? Write down your top ten choices. You can turn your choices into a book just like this one. Search the Internet or magazines for pictures. Print or cut them out to fill the pages. Or draw your own!

KANSAS BY MAP

> MAP KEY

- 🟉 Capital city
- ◯ City
- ◎ Point of interest
- 🔺 Highest elevation
- –·– State border

S M O K Y

COLORADO

🔺 Mount Sunflower
(4,039 feet/
1,231 m)

G R E A T

G

Arkansas River

Miles
0   20   40   60
0   40   80
Kilometers

KANSAS

Visit www.lerneresource.com to learn
more about the state flag of Kansas.

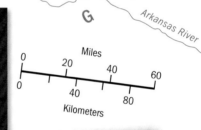

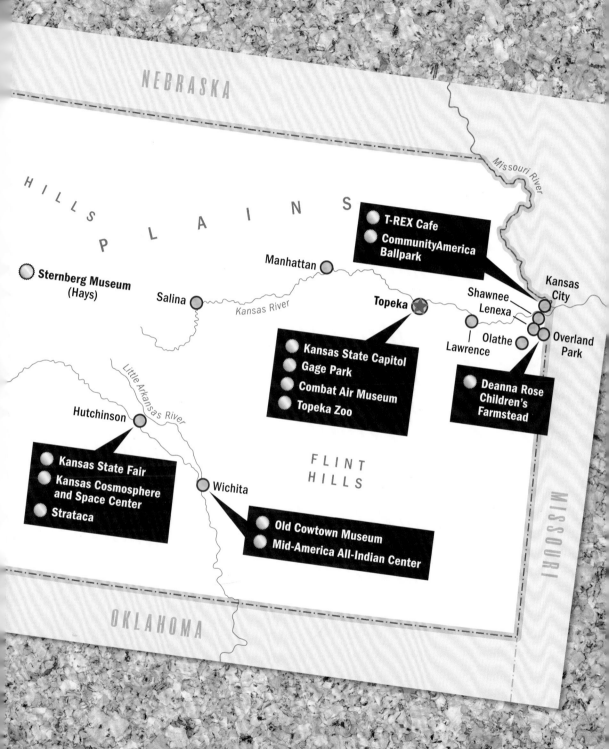

NEBRASKA

HILLS

PLAINS

Missouri River

Sternberg Museum
(Hays)

Manhattan

Salina

Kansas River

Topeka

T-REX Cafe

CommunityAmerica
Ballpark

Kansas
City

Shawnee
Lenexa

Lawrence

Olathe

Overland
Park

Kansas State Capitol

Gage Park

Combat Air Museum

Topeka Zoo

Deanna Rose
Children's
Farmstead

Little Arkansas River

Hutchinson

Kansas State Fair

Kansas Cosmosphere
and Space Center

Strataca

Wichita

FLINT
HILLS

Old Cowtown Museum

Mid-America All-Indian Center

MISSOURI

OKLAHOMA

27

KANSAS FACTS

NICKNAMES: The Sunflower State, the Jayhawk State, the Wheat State

SONG: "Home on the Range," words by Brewster Higley and music by Daniel Kelley

MOTTO: *Ad astra per aspera*, or "To the stars through difficulties"

> **FLOWER:** sunflower

TREE: cottonwood

> **BIRD:** western meadowlark

ANIMAL: American bison

FOOD: chicken fried steak

DATE AND RANK OF STATEHOOD: January 29, 1861; the 34th state

> **CAPITAL:** Topeka

AREA: 82,274 square miles (213,089 sq. km)

AVERAGE JANUARY TEMPERATURE: 30°F (–1°C)

AVERAGE JULY TEMPERATURE: 80°F (27°C)

POPULATION AND RANK: 2,893,957; 34th (2013)

MAJOR CITIES AND POPULATIONS: Wichita (386,552), Overland Park (181,260), Kansas City (148,483), Olathe (131,885), Topeka (127,679), Lawrence (90,811)

NUMBER OF US CONGRESS MEMBERS: 4 representatives, 2 senators

NUMBER OF ELECTORAL VOTES: 6

NATURAL RESOURCES: gypsum, helium, limestone, natural gas, petroleum, salt

> **AGRICULTURAL PRODUCTS:** cattle, corn for grain, hogs, soybeans, wheat

MANUFACTURED GOODS: aircraft, aircraft parts, camping equipment, missiles

STATE HOLIDAYS AND CELEBRATIONS: Amelia Earhart Festival, Kansas Day, Kansas Sampler Festival, Kansas State Fair, Symphony in the Flint Hills

GLOSSARY

cockpit: the area in the front of an airplane or spacecraft where the pilot sits

dwelling: a building or structure where people live

frontier: an unsettled area where few people live

hangar: a large building where airplanes and helicopters are kept

meteor: a piece of rock or metal from space that falls to Earth so quickly it forms a streak of light

pioneer: related to one of the first people to live in a new territory

saloon: a bar where people buy drinks

FURTHER INFORMATION

Flint Hills Discovery Center
http://www.flinthillsdiscovery.org
Read about cool geology, biology, and cultural exhibits and activities for kids and families at the Flint Hills in Kansas.

Glaser, Jason. *Kansas: The Sunflower State*. New York: PowerKids Press, 2010. Learn about major events in Kansas's history and what makes the state great.

Ingram, W. Scott. *Kansas*. New York: Children's Press, 2009. Learn about how Kansas fits into American history.

Kansas Kids
http://www.kssos.org/resources/kansas_kids.html
Test your Kansas knowledge with crossword puzzles, mazes, and fun games.

Tallgrass Prairie National Preserve
http://www.nps.gov/tapr/forkids/index.htm
Learn about the tallgrass prairie that used to cover much of North America, including Kansas.

Walker, Sally M. *Figuring Out Fossils*. Minneapolis: Lerner Publications, 2013. Learn all about the science of fossils and what they can tell us about the world.

INDEX

American Indians, 9, 22, 23

Atlantic Ocean, 14

Bosin, Francis "Blackbear," 23

Cinemoo Theater, 10

Combat Air Museum, 14

CommunityAmerica Park, 8

Deanna Rose Children's Farmstead, 10

Earhart, Amelia, 14

Fish-Within-a-Fish, 24

Gage Park, 12

Hutchinson, 6, 16, 20

Kansas City, 8, 18

Kansas City T-Bones, 8

Kansas Cosmosphere and Space Center, 4, 6

Kansas State Fair, 4, 16

Keeper of the Plains, 23

Mid-America All-Indian Center, 22

Mollett Early Space Flight Gallery, 6

Old Cowtown Museum, 22, 23

Overland Park, 10

Salt Mine Express, 20

Sternberg Museum, 24

Stratatca, 20

Topeka, 12, 14

Topeka Zoo, 12

T-REX Cafe, 18

Wichita, 22, 23

PHOTO ACKNOWLEDGMENTS

The images in this book are used with the permission of: © Ricardo Reitmeyer/Thinkstock, p. 1; NASA, pp. 2–3; © Ratchapol Yindeesuk /Shutterstock Images, p. 4; © Ricardo Reitmeyer /Shutterstock Images, p. 5 (top); © Laura Westlund /Independent Picture Service, pp. 5 (bottom), 26–27; © Kansas Cosmosphere, pp. 6–7, 7 (right); © Harry Frank/iStock/Thinkstock, p. 7 (left); © stevekc CC 2.0, pp. 8–9; © Pamela Burley /iStock/Thinkstock, p. 9 (top); © North Wind Picture Archives/Alamy, p. 9 (bottom); © City of Overland Park CC 2.0, pp. 10–11, 10; © Everett Collection /Shutterstock Images, p. 11; © The Topeka Capital Journal, Anthony S. Bush/AP Images, pp. 12–13 © Wiratchai Wansamngam/Shutterstock Images, p. 13 (top); © The Editorialist/Alamy, p. 13 (bottom); © Charlie Riedel/AP Images, pp. 14–15; Harris and Ewing/Library of Congress, p. 14 (LC-DIG-hec-40747); © Ivan Cholakov/Shutterstock Images, p. 15; © Joel Sartore/Alamy, pp. 16–17; © Lindsey Bauman/AP Images, p. 17 (left); © Wasan Srisawat/Shutterstock Images, p. 17 (right); © Bill Grant/Alamy, pp. 18–19; © Ayleen Gaspar, p. 19 (left); © Tom Uhlenbrock/Newscom, p. 19 (right); © Larry W. Smith/EPA/Newscom, pp. 20–21; © Dan Leeth/Alamy, p. 21 (left); © iStock/Thinkstock, p. 21 (right); © Walter Bibikow/Danita Delimont Photography/Newscom, pp. 22–23; © Mark and Audrey Gibson/Alamy, p. 22; © Allen Graham/Shutterstock Images, p. 23; © Tom Dorsey/AP Images, pp. 24–25; © Allen Holder/Newscom, p. 24; © James St. John CC 2.0, p. 25; © nicoolay/iStockphoto, p. 26; © Purestock /Thinkstock, p. 29 (top); © Photography by J.H. Williams/iStock/Thinkstock, p. 29 (middle left); © Philip Scalia/Alamy, p. 29 (middle right); © Fuse /Thinkstock, p. 29 (bottom).

Front cover: © Ricardo Reitmeyer/Shutterstock.com (statue); © iStockphoto.com/Trout55 (sunflowers); © Joel Sartore/National Geographic Image Collection/Alamy (state fair); © iStockphoto.com/ flammulated (meadowlark); © Laura Westlund/ Independent Picture Service (map); © iStockphoto.com/fpm (seal); © iStockphoto. com/vicm (pushpins); © iStockphoto.com/benz190 (corkboard).